VIRGINIA POLYTECHNIC INSTITUTE AND STATE UNIVERSITY

THEN and NOW
VIRGINIA TECH

PHOTOGRAPHED BY
CHARLES SHOFFNER

HARMONY HOUSE
PUBLISHERS-LOUISVILLE

Executive Editors: William Butler and William Strode
Library of Congress Catalog Number: 90-81404
Hardcover International Standard Book Number 0-916509-78-8
Printed by D.W. Friesen & Sons Ltd., Manitoba, Canada
Separations by Gateway Press, Inc., Louisville, Kentucky
First Edition printed February, 1991 by Harmony House Publishers,
P.O. Box 90, Prospect, Kentucky 40059 (502) 228-2010 / 228-4446
Copyright © 1991 by Harmony House Publishers
Photographs copyright © 1991 by Charles Shoffner

This book or portions thereof may not be reproduced in any form without permission of Harmony House Publishers. Photographs may not be reproduced in any form without permission of Charles Shoffner.

Performing Arts Building

PROLOGUE

Virginia Tech's campus echoes with history . . . more than 118 years and 100,000 alumni. We are a university that was born in the lengthened shadow of the Civil War. Ours is a university dedicated, even then, to regeneration. Ours is a university dedicated to the potential, to the hopes, to the unity, and to the life of tomorrow.

"Tomorrow" is now here. Tomorrow belongs to people. In one recent five-year period Virginia Tech faculty members received 508 national and international honors. Honors are our reflection; they are not our reason for being. However, excellence is; service is; and nearly 23,000 students are. Those students are our tomorrow.

These academic halls, these buildings, and these biographies are all filled with purpose. It is a purpose dedicated to the life of scholarship and service. We are not an assembly line that produces commodities called graduates. We will not pour education into a mold or convert it into a computer program. We will concede that university values do not begin and end with excellent works published in excellent jounals and read only by excellent minds. Scholarship is part of our honor . . . part of our pride . . . and part of any great university's future.

It has been said that, "It is history that teaches us to hope." Thus, we came to honor history in our dedication and determination to find tomorrow. Our College of Architecture is building that future. And a national publication has said simply that this college "is one of the nation's best." Engineering's forward-looking undergraduate program is in the nation's top 10. So are programs in a revitalized College of Agriculture and Life Sciences. Among Business Colleges earning national rankings is ours. The preeminent Marketing Education program in America is also ours. So is one of the best Child Development programs in the nation, a program nurtured and developed in our own College of Human Resources. The College of Arts and Sciences is a masterwork of diversity and creativity with instruction and instructors recognized as among the best anywhere. Our College of Education helps prepare young minds to challenge the minds of their future students in all walks of professional education. And, the College of Veterinary Medicine looks forward to the continued advances in animal care and medical research that unfold each day.

Tomorrow is here, and we look toward horizons instead of walls. Our vision extends to generations. So, on a clear day, we can see 100 years or more. And all of us can see tomorrow. For tomorrow offers so much . . . in the maroon and burnt orange . . . in the excellence and in the service . . . in a university called Virginia Tech.

James D. McComas
President

Hillcrest Hall

INTRODUCTION

We continue to build upon our past. The people I have known here at Virginia Tech helped to lay a strong foundation for what has followed, an unprecedented growth and development at one of Virginia's major universities. I remember the day the Board of Visitors decided to add "and State University" to the name of our school. There seemed to be no better way to describe the VPI that had added several new colleges and had already attained the broad breadth of a university.

My recollections of the past forty-five years are stored in my mind like carefully drawn etchings. The Drillfield was a huge lawn with large castles surrounding it. At least that is the way I remember it as a boy of only fourteen years of age attending my first 4-H Short Course. Then to come here as a student and be assigned to the Radford Arsenal barracks was a bit of a shock! This was the period during the late forties when a large number of veterans returned to college on the G.I. Bill.

Some of my early acquaintances on campus are still contributing to the vibrant life of this community called Blacksburg. Forrest Rollins (Algebra), Roy Blaser (Forage Crops), Burke Johnston (Administration), Mike Kipps (Crops), Sam Obenshain (Soils), Clarice Slusher Pritchard (Registrar), and Lyle Kinnear (Psychology) are some of the stalwarts who influenced my life more than I realized until now. Others who have passed on but remain vividly in my mind and heart are Walter Newman, (Uncle Walter handed me my scholarship), George Litton, Ralph Hunt and Bill Daughtrey. Friends like these remain with us forever.

Like Burke Johnston, I take great pleasure in seeing buildings on campus named for these great individuals! They were not only dedicated to learning and service to mankind, but they had special personalities which enabled them to influence people beyond their usual ambitions. May God bless them all.

In addition to professors and buildings, alumni usually ask me about Tech sports and the weather. The athletic program has grown by leaps and bounds with the influx of women in the seventies. We now have seven varsity sports for women and eleven for men. Women's teams compete in cross country, volleyball, basketball, indoor track, swimming, outdoor track, and tennis. Tech competes in the Metro Conference in all sports except football. Hopefully, Tech will soon be in an all-sports conference.

Now, about the weather, you can probably guess what my answer will be. It has often been said in jest, if you don't like the weather, just wait a while and it will change! Believe me, the seasons are still very distinct in Blacksburg. The spring, summer and fall are just great, but the winter still gets to most of us. There is nothing that will compare to a brisk walk across the Drillfield in midwinter to wake one up in the morning!

In spite of a little chilly weather and a few setbacks in athletics, Tech is making some wonderful progress. The changes in our academic capabilities since the mid-forties are mind-boggling by any stretch of the imagination. Who would have thought back then that Virginia Tech would have nearly 23,000 students with more than 4,000 graduate students, enrolled in eight different colleges. Our peer universities now include Cornell University, Pennsylvania State University and Michigan State University. Virginia Tech now ranks seventeenth in the nation in national merit scholars. We are an outstanding university!

As an alumnus, I have found it easy to get excited about the future of Virginia Tech. I'm sure there are many reasons why one chooses to get involved with our University, but the primary one for me was the solid foundation that already existed when I arrived here. The poet John Masefield described how I feel about my University:

THE UNIVERSITY

There are few earthly things more beautiful than a University.

It is a place where those who hate ignorance may strive to know; where those who perceive truth may strive to make others see; where seekers and learners alike, banded together in the search for knowledge will honor thought in all its finer ways, will welcome thinkers in distress or in exile, will uphold ever the dignity of thought and learning and will exact standards in these things.

They give to the young in their

Alumni Hall

impressionable years, the bond of a lofty purpose shared, of a great corporate life whose links will not be loosed until they die.

They give young people that close companionship for which youth longs, and that chance of the endless, without which youth would seem a waste of time . . ."

As expressed by current Provost Carlisle, "the University is a gateway: it is a gateway inward for some previously excluded and a gateway outward, out into the global society." Four or five years studying and interrelating with students from many lands and various walks of life can be a tremendous education. If only we had the opportunity to do it again. Many of us would have a totally different outlook . . . we would not be thinking so much about what a course or lab means to us personally, but what it could mean to our community and our ability to make improvments in living for people in general.

The Alumni Association will continue to help enhance the quality of learning and student life at the University. Through the Association, every alum will have an opportunity to be heard and to contribute something back. When you think about it, the public has come to depend on Alumni Associations to provide the margin of excellence.

Quality, or current strengths, have to be nurtured with continuous planning and adapting for the future. Most of this work is done without fanfare and behind the scenes. Of course, if you look, you can see studies, discussions and various kinds of research taking place when you visit the campus. It is going on all the time in every department and college. Like a well-functioning business, a university must be competitive in all its programs because you and I are its "product" and we must all compete with graduates from other universities.

World-class academic reputations aren't easily cultivated in a university. State funding has helped to bring faculty salaries up to a competitive level, but it takes more to be ranked among the nation's best. Our alumni have made the difference! They have devoted generously at times to fund professorships and other means of recognizing excellence in teaching and scholarship.

Quoting Eugene Rowe, class of 1933, "the best legacy one can leave Virginia Tech is to invite the continued interests of her outstanding students as they move into their chosen work." I learned a great deal from Gene Rowe — his philosophy of staying involved with one's alma mater has served me well. Trying to emulate such a man is challenging to say the least, but I have tried to follow his example. My career here at Virginia Tech has been devoted largely to getting our alumni involved.

Some of the happiest people I have known are those like Gene Rowe who get deeply involved in volunteerism. They find few financial rewards but plenty of "mental wages," those psychological benefits that are far more valuable and lasting. As non-paid volunteers, alumni can do things the paid staff cannot. It is important to tell legislators that higher education is crucial to the state's progress. It is important to tell newspaper editors what is going right within the University. As graduates, it is very important that we tell high school students the value of a degree earned at our alma mater.

The motto of our University is "Ut Prosim," which translated means "that I may serve." Let us unite in using our minds and resources to be the best we can be. Our University needs her alumni to unite with faculty and staff to continue working for improvements that will move us toward excellence. While some are worrying about *The Closing of the American Mind*, (the book by Allan Bloom) we can commit ourselves to opening those minds!

With our beautiful campus and all the talent residing here, we can have a revival in that traditional American value of "opportunity for all." This *can* be a better world, and what better way to begin than with our youth. Through our teaching, extension and research programs we can reach anyone who wishes to get involved.

George E. (Buddy) Russell
Vice President for Alumni Relations
Virginia Tech

VIRGINIA TECH: A SELECTED CHRONOLOGY

1851 Olin and Preston Institute opens
1862 Morrill Land Grant Act becomes law (July 2)
1864 Morrill Act accepted for Virginia by "Unionist" legislature
1869 Preston and Olin Institute chartered with collegiate powers
1872 Bill establishing V.A.M.C. signed (March 19); First meeting of Board of Visitors (March 25-26); Montgomery County citizens approve bond issue (May 24); Charles L.C. Minor elected first president (August 14); First session begins (October 1)
1873 First social fraternity charted at V.A.M.C.
1875 Twelve students awarded first non-degree diplomas; Alumni Association established; First student publication, the *Gray Jacket*, published
1876 First off-campus student trip (to Richmond)
1879 John L. Buchanan elected second president
1880 Social fraternities banned
1882 Thomas N. Conrad elected third president; Military system firmly established
1883 First degrees (Bachelor of Arts) awarded
1886 Lindsay L. Lomax elected fourth president; Agricultural Experiment Station legally established
1891 John M. McBryde elected fifth president; Athletic Association organized; Alumni Association reorganized with a newly drawn constitution; Corps of Cadets established as a permanent organization
1892 First Bachelor of Science and Master of Science awarded; First football game played
1895 First yearbook published, entitled *The Bugle*
1896 "Polytechnic Institute" added to name of the College; Chicago Maroon and Burnt Orange adopted as official colors; "Ut Prosim" chosen as official motto
1903 First dean named (E.A. Smyth, dean of the faculty)
1904 First summer school held
1907 Graduate Department established; Paul B. Barringer elected sixth president
1909 First basketball game played
1913 Joseph D. Eggleston becomes seventh president
1914 Agricultural Extension Division established
1917 First R.O.T.C. unit established
1919 Julian A. Burruss becomes eighth president
1920 Quality credit and credit hour system established
1921 Engineering Experiment Station established; Women admitted for first time as full-time students
1922 Semi-Centennial celebration
1923 Engineering Extension Division established; First woman student receives degree (Mary E. Brumfield)
1925 Future Farmers of Virginia (later FFA) founded at V.P.I.
1928 First Homecoming Day designated by the Alumni Association
1930 First extension branch established in Richmond; Civilian Student Union formed
1942 First Doctor of Philosophy awarded
1944 Radford State Teachers College becomes V.P.I., Women's Division; "Agricultural and Mechanical College" dropped from college name
1945 John R. Hutcheson elected ninth president
1946 Walter S. Newman elected first vice president; "Rad-Tech" campus established; Civilians outnumber cadets for first time
1947 Walter S. Newman elected ninth president
1948 V.P.I. Educational Foundation, Inc., established
1949 "Rad-Tech" campus closed
1950 Student Aid Association chartered to provide athletic scholarships
1952 Cooperative Education Program established
1962 T. Marshall Hahn, Jr., becomes eleventh president
1963 First student to win Rhodes Scholarship (William W. Lewis, Jr.); Won first (and only) Southern Conference football championship
1964 Corps of Cadets becomes voluntary option; V.P.I.- Radford merger dissolved

1965	Bachelor of Arts degree re-instated; University withdraws from Southern Conference
1966	Cadets and civilians unite to form one student government; University-wide Extension and Research Divisions established
1968	First student representation on University Council
1969	Faculty Senate established; Northern Virginia Graduate Center established in Reston
1970	"and State University" added to V.P.I.'s name
1972	Centennial Year; Bachelor of Technology approved (effective Fall) Recognized social fraternity-sorority system approved
1973	First Doctor of Education awarded; Women admitted into the Corps of Cadets for the first time in fall quarter; Tech wins NIT basketball tournament; Academy of Teaching Excellence established
1974	Tech's first civilian marching band, the Marching Virginians, makes its debut in the fall; First dean of veterinary medicine (R.B. Talbot) appointed to plan the University's first professional college
1975	William E. Lavery becomes twelfth president
1976	Office of Provost established; Probate of John Lee Pratt's will reveals bequest to Tech which would amount to approximately $11.5 million for engineering and animal nutrition programs; First athletic scholarships offered to women
1978	Tech joins the Metro Athletic Conference; Kylene Barker '78 named "Miss America" 1979
1979	Full-time enrollment tops 20,000 for the first time
1980	First class of College of Veterinary Medicine enrolled
1983	First student member (non-voting) of Board of Visitors (James Stroh) appointed; First on-campus fraternity-sorority houses completed; Blacksburg bus system begins operations, primarily funded by $4 per quarter per-student assessment
1984	First D.V.M. degrees presented in June; $50-million "Campaign for Excellence" begins; College of Veterinary Medicine's Marion duPont Scott Equine Medical Center opened in Leesburg, Virginia
1985	Board of Visitors approved change from quarter to semester calendar to begin in 1988; Corporate Research Center established; Virginia Tech Intellectual Properties, Inc. formed to receive and manage patents and copyrights on behalf of the university
1986	Cranwell International Center dedicated and opened; Campaign for Excellence ended, more than doubling the goal by receiving $117 million in contributions; Robert B. Pamplin, Sr. and Robert B. Pamplin, Jr. donated $10 million to the College of Business which was renamed the R.B. Pamplin College of Business; The Harvey W. Peters Research Center for the Study of Parkinson's Disease established by a $3 million gift from Marion Bradley Via
1987	Football team won Peach Bowl, defeating N.C. State 25-24; Renovation of President's Home, "The Grove," began; Tech signed a $7.6 million contract with I.B.M. for a new telecommunication system for the Blacksburg campus and Northern Virginia Graduate Center
1988	James D. McComas became thirteenth president; Semester system begun; Tech assumed responsibility for management of Graduate Education Center of the Roanoke Valley; Biochemistry and Nutrition Building renamed Engel Hall in honor of Reuben W. Engel, first department head of biochemistry and nutrition; Renovation of Solitude begun
1989	Hotel Roanoke donated to Tech by Norfolk-Southern Corporation; Virginia Cooperative Extension Service reorganized
1990	"Second Century Campaign" started to raise $17 million for Tech athletics

Pamplin Hall

Preceding page; Campus view including McBryde Hall

Newman Library

East Eggleston Hall

Duck Pond

Overleaf; Aerial view of Upper Quad

University Club

THE EARLY YEARS

Virginia Agricultural and Mechanical College, as shown in an 1890 engraving. (The name was changed to VPI in 1896).

A view of the campus and grounds, 1896. Left to right: Second Academic Building, Barracks No. 1, First Academic Building and the Commandant's Quarters.

J.M. McBryde, the fifth president.

The President's house, 1899. This building was later incorporated as a wing of Henderson Hall, the present infirmary.

Mess and Commencement Hall, 1896.

The campus, 1900. Left to right: Faculty Row, YMCA Building (under construction), the Barracks and Academic Buildings.

The Preston and Olin Building, the first and only building on campus when the Virginia Agricultural and Mechanical College opened in 1872.

No. 1 Barracks, 1922, (now Lane Hall).

Cadet Corps in formation, 1896.

Agricultural Hall, 1909, now known as Price Hall.

The YMCA Building, now the Performing Arts Building, 1901.

The town of Blacksburg from the top of the Shops Building, 1901.

The interior of the Library, 1917.

The Maury Literary Society quarters on the second floor of the Second Academic Building, 1900.

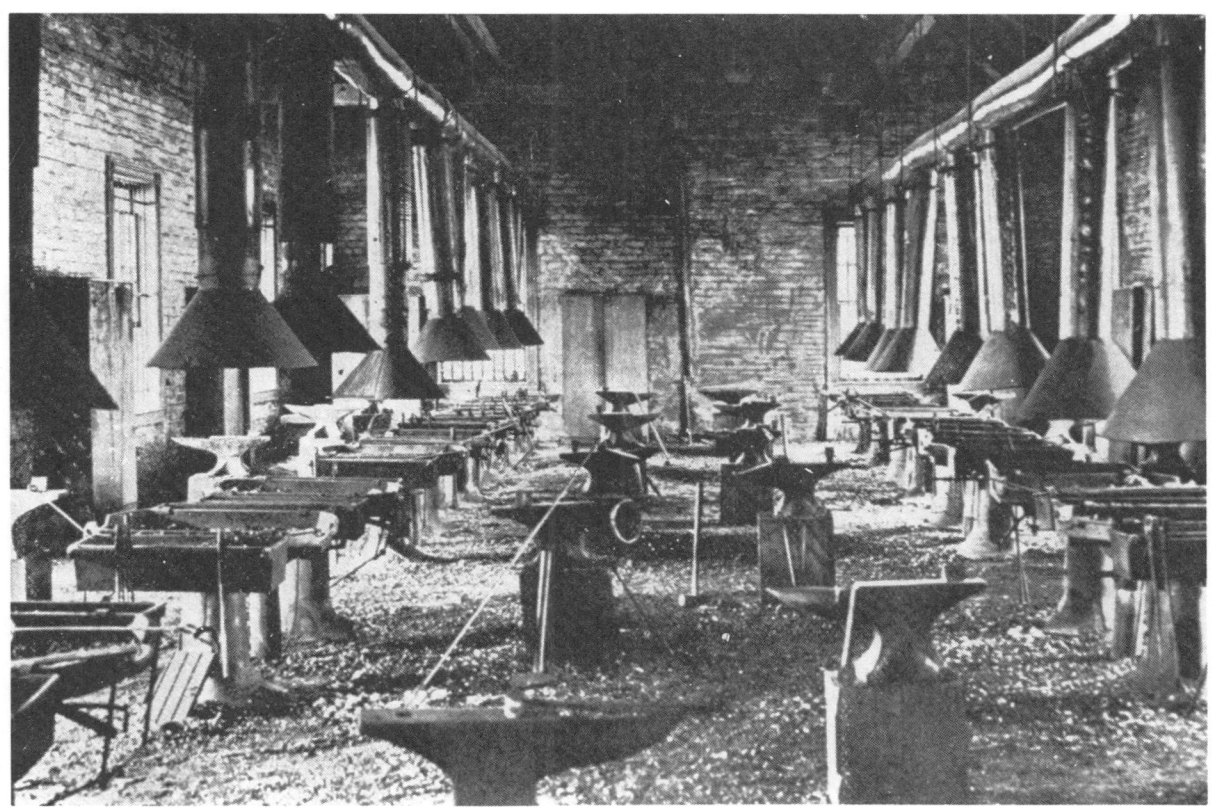

The Forge Shop, 1895.

Old Science Hall burns down, 1904

A fire drill at Barracks No. 3, 1908.

THE UNIVERSITY TODAY
VIRGINIA TECH

The university instills within each member of the university community an appreciation of the values and obligations of productive citizenship and the responsibilities of leadership while promoting personal and intellectual development . . . as the university moves toward the year 2000, it will identify and build on strengths across the university, forge innovative and mutually productive relationships with industry and government, manage resources efficiently, and establish a clear identity as a forward-thinking, high quality institution that systematically guides and evaluates its future.

From the University Mission Statement

Memorial Chapel

The Grove, the President's Home

Main Eggleston Hall

Computer Aided Design

Surveying Class

Chemistry Class

Architecture Lab

Agriculture

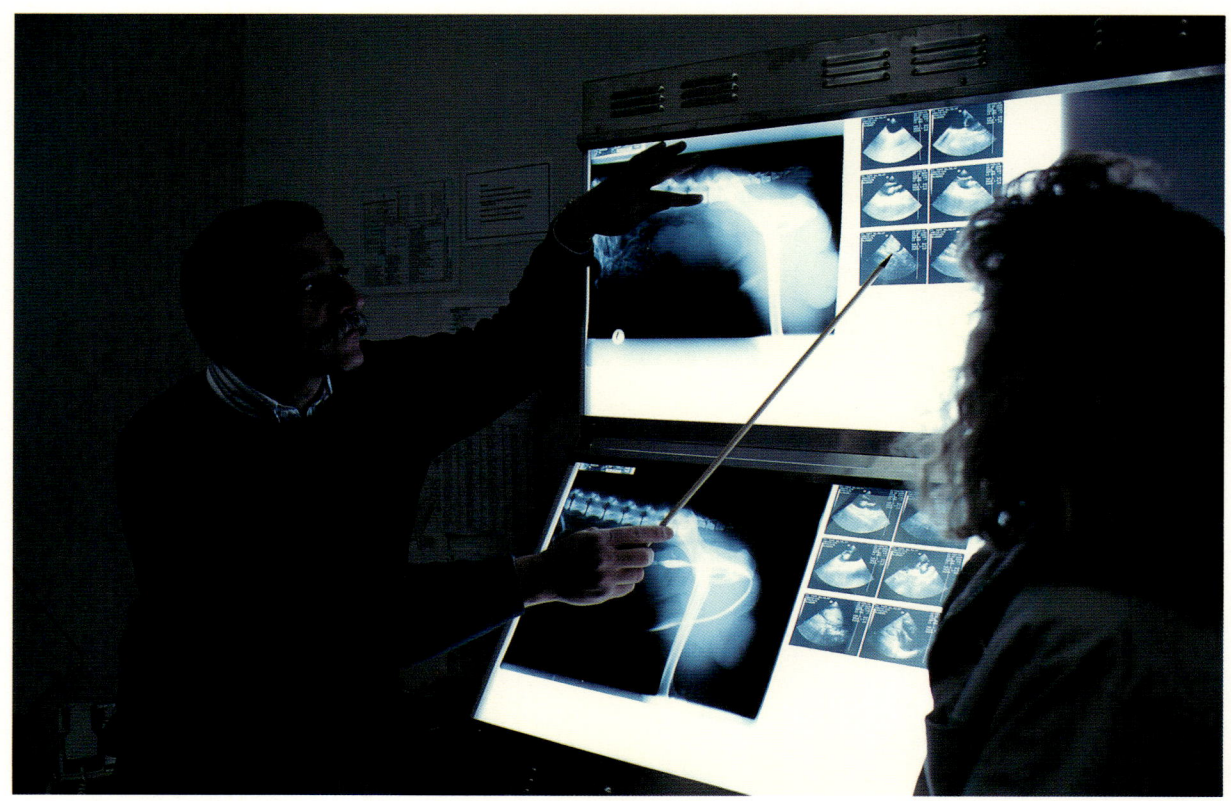

Veterinary Medicine

Entomology Class

Entering the Alumni Gateway, 1922. These gates were removed in 1936.

The growing campus, 1916.

Dr. Julian A. Burruss, the eighth president, 1928.

The campus continues to grow — this shot is from 1947.

The Administration Building ("The Rock House"), circa 1905.

Stone Dormitory (Campbell Hall), 1936.

The World War I Memorial Monument, left, beside the First Academic Building, 1936.

Lover's Lane, 1928.

The College walk between the academic buildings.

Davidson Hall, 1936.

Original McBryde Hall, 1928.

VAMC Cadet Band, 1894, in front of the Second Academic Building.

Cadets saluting statue of Rankin, considered the "Father of modern engineering," in Patton Hall.

Hillcrest Dormitory, the women's dorm, in 1942.

The "trailer camp" for returning G.I.s, 1946. This was located beside the Duck Pond.

THE UNIVERSITY EXPERIENCE
VIRGINIA TECH

Despite the geographic and economic diversity of Tech's student body, students do share some characteristics. They tend to be friendly, active, and outgoing. They're serious about their academic studies and their career goals. And by the time they graduate, they have developed a strong sense of pride — in themselves and in Virginia Tech.

Homecoming

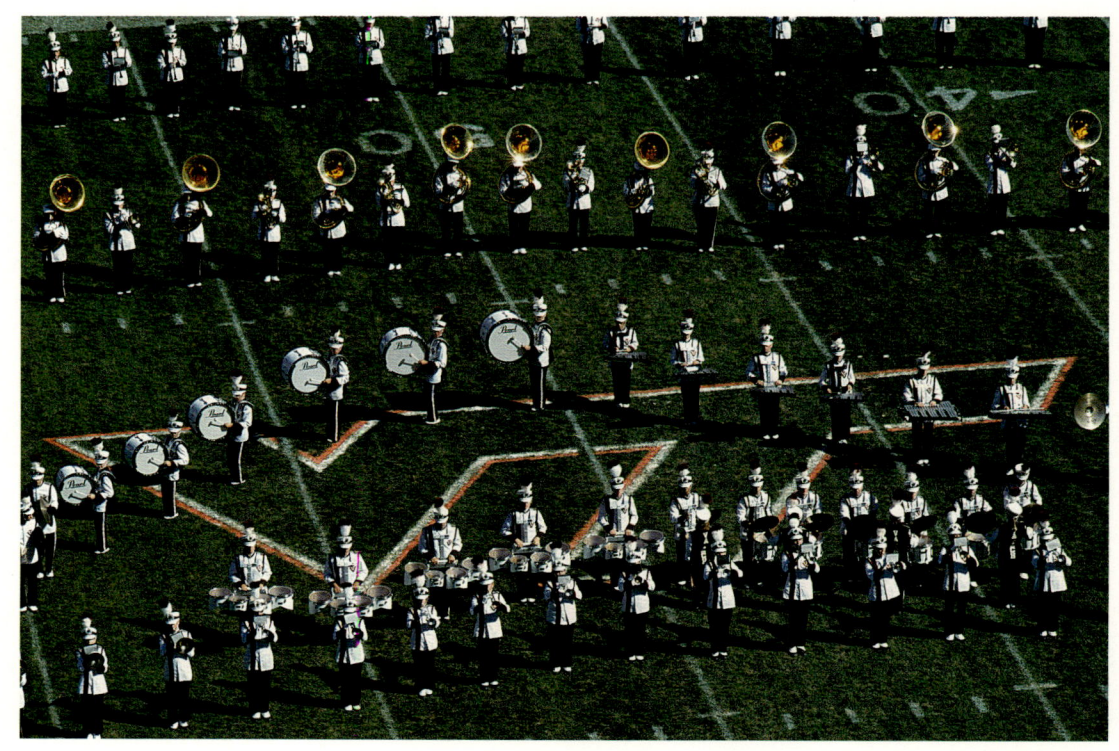

89

Cassell Coliseum

Lane Hall, Old No. 1 Barracks

Graduation, Lane Stadium

Four women were first admitted as students in 1921; another, Mary Brumfield, left, was a transfer student who received her B.S. in 1923. Pictured with her at the 1925 graduation exercises are (left to right) Ruth Terrett, Lucy Lee Lancaster, Louise Jacobs and Carrie Sibold. (Brumfield received an M.S. degree at this graduation).

Annual Rat Snow Battle on the Drill Field, 1908.

A Rat-upperclassmen football game, 1949.

An Alumni Association reunion, 1917.
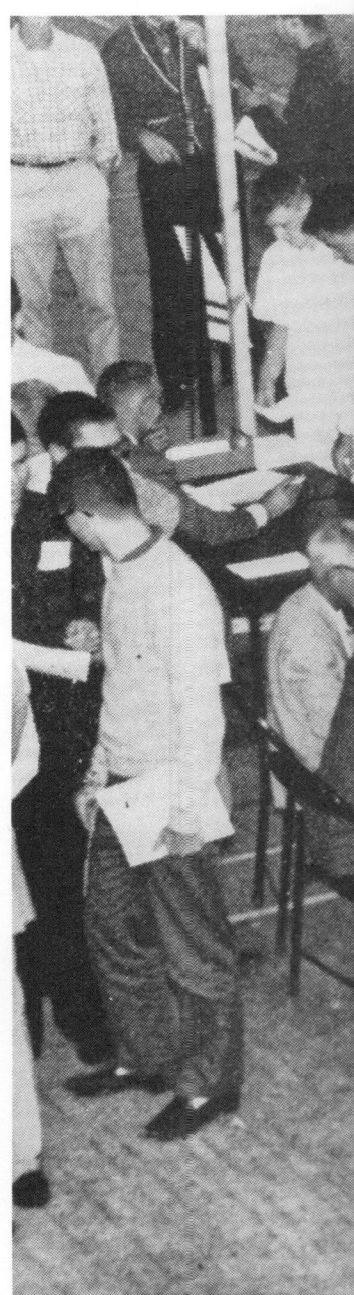

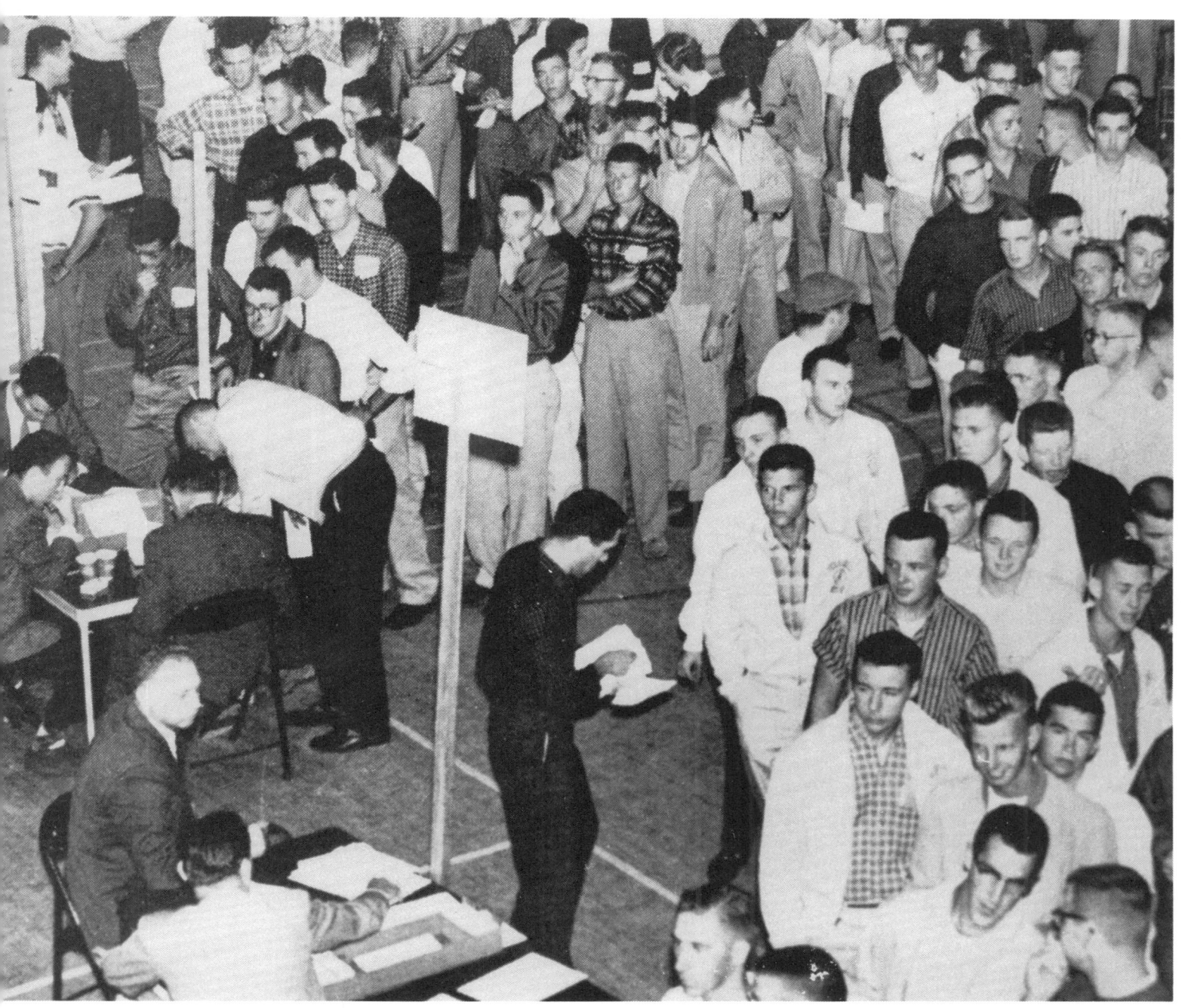
Class registration, 1959.

The college's first formally organized baseball team, 1892.

This 1895 football team went 4-1 on the season, losing only to VMI 10-6.

A record-breaking crowd of 13,000 squeezed into Miles Stadium to see the Gobblers beat previously unbeaten N.C. State 14-6 in 1947.

A pole-vaulter on the track team uses a bamboo pole, 1917.

Varsity baseball, 1917.

The first-ever float parade at Homecoming, 1948.

1942 cheerleaders Bob Stanley and Glen Chase.

Football star Ron Casto hauls in a pass in a 1950 game.

A pre-game fracas at the annual VPI-VMI Thanksgiving Day football game, 1964.

The Ring Dance, 1941.

A ribbon dance, 1942.

The VPI Cavaliers, a dance band, was organized in 1946 for campus entertainment. This photo is from 1947.

Bandleader Glen Gray at Mid-Winters, 1950.

Harry James and his Orchestra at a Cotillion Club dance, 1958.

That I may serve